Railways & Recollections
Bournemouth: the station and shed area
Gavin Morrison

© Gavin Morrison 2019

All rights reserved. No part of this publication may be reproduced, stored in a retrieval system or transmitted, in any form or by any means, electronic, mechanical, photocopying, recording or otherwise, without prior permission in writing from Silver Link Publishing Ltd.

First published in 2019

British Library Cataloguing in Publication Data

A catalogue record for this book is available from the British Library.

ISBN 978 1 85794 538 6

Silver Link Publishing Ltd
The Trundle
Ringstead Road
Great Addington
Kettering
Northants NN14 4BW

Tel/Fax: 01536 330588
email: sales@nostalgiacollection.com
Website: www.nostalgiacollection.com

Printed and bound in the Czech Republic

Title page This impressive line-up shows three rebuilt 'Merchant Navies' outside the shed, Nos 35014 *Nederland Line*, 35026 *Lamport & Holt Line* and 35023 *Holland-Afrika Line*. 6 September 1964

Front cover: At the east end of the station rebuilt 'Merchant Navy' No 35026 *Lamport & Holt Line*' is seen departing with an up express for Waterloo on 10 September 1964.

Contents

Introduction	2
The photographs	4
Bournemouth shed: codes and allocations, 1950, 1959 and 1965	62-63
Index of locomotive classes	64

Introduction

Bournemouth's fine station was opened on 20 July 1885 and was designed by the London & South Western Railway's chief engineer William Jacob. It replaced the original station named Bournemouth East, which was situated on the other side of the main road at the east end and had opened in 1870. The name Bournemouth East was kept until it became Bournemouth Central in 1899, the name it retained until 1967 when the other station in the town, Bournemouth West, closed with the ending of steam services. It then became just Bournemouth, which it remains today.

Prior to the Grouping the station had dealings with five other railways: the South Western Railway, the Southampton & Dorchester Railway, the Ringwood, Christchurch & Bournemouth Railway, the Salisbury & Dorset Junction Railway, and the Somerset & Dorset Joint Railway.

The journey of 108 miles and 2 chains to London Waterloo has been the main traffic over the years, but what are now known as CrossCountry services expanded considerably to all parts of the UK. In steam-operated days most services continued to West station, where the carriage maintenance facilities existed, while others continued through to Weymouth.

The steam shed was originally at the East station, but this closed in 1883 when a new one was built at the west end of the present station. It was expanded again in 1888. Further extensions took place in 1921, then complete rebuilding happened between 1936 and 1938, when a 65-foot turntable was installed.

It was always a very cramped and difficult shed to operate, and proposals were put forward to relocate it at Branksome, but these never materialised, and the pre-war layout continued to the end of steam in 1967.

I well remember going to Bournemouth on

A year before the end of steam Type 3s (later Class 33s) worked frequently on the Bournemouth-Waterloo expresses. No D6501 (later No 33002) is ready to leave the station with an up express. 31 July 1966

holiday just after nationalisation and spending most of the time at the station. It seemed that every late afternoon they would reorganise the position of the engines on the shed for their next duties and almost all were pulled out of the shed and shunted into position, so there was no need to make any effort to try and get round – all this could easily be observed from the station platform.

I still have my rather disorganised 'spotting' book from that summer, which tells me that I saw 23 different 'King Arthurs', about 30 different 'M7s', 14 different 'Lord Nelsons' – almost the whole class – eight different 'Q' 0-6-0s, six 'Merchant Navies', five 'West Country'/'Battle of Britain' 'Pacifics', and plenty of 'T9s', 'Moguls' and other classes.

I vividly remember most of the locos still running in the Malachite green, but for some reason I don't seem to remember the 'Pacifics'. Only one LMS engine off the S&DJR was seen, and that was the now preserved 4F No 4422.

The big change came in 1967 when electrification reached Bournemouth. The steam shed obviously closed and the two lines through the centre of the station were removed. As already mentioned, Bournemouth West station also closed, but the carriage facilities remained open for repairs and servicing.

The electric services were operated by EMUs known as 4REPs for the powered units and 4TCs for the non-powered ones. These were hauled on to Weymouth by Class 33/1s in a push-pull operation. Other services were diesel-hauled. This operation continued until the introduction of the 'Wessex Electrics' (Class 442s), which came into service when the electrification of the line through to Weymouth was completed. These fine EMUs were cascaded to the 'Gatwick Express' services upon the introduction of new Class 444 and 450 EMUs. Their days on the Gatwick services have since ended, but they are being refurbished again for further use.

The station was badly damaged in the storm of 1987 and remained in very bad condition until it was sorted out by Network Rail in 2000. Services today are now operated by South West Trains and CrossCountry. It is a very busy station, with passenger numbers in 2012/13 of 2.505 million per annum, which increased to 2.756 million in 2016/17.

I trust this book will give some indication of what it was like in the latter days of steam operation, which is now more than 50 years ago. How time flies!

Gavin Morrison

Bournemouth shed had a small allocation of the Maunsell 'Q' Class 0-6-0s from the 1950s to the early 1960s. No 30536 is on the shed fitted with a standard chimney. 22 April 1962

Another 'Q' Class on shed that day was No 30541, which still retains the multiple-jet blastpipe with a squat chimney. This was an attempt by Bulleid to improve the performance of the 20 members of the class. 22 April 1962

The last 'Merchant Navy' to be built in 1949 was No 35030 *Elder-Dempster Lines*. It was rebuilt in March 1958 and lasted to the end of Southern Region steam in July 1967. 9 June 1963

The unrebuilt 'West Country' and 'Battle of Britain' Classes were a familiar sight on Bournemouth shed for more than 20 years until the end of steam in July 1967. No 34061 *73 Squadron* (originally numbered 21C161) is awaiting its next duty on the shed. 9 June 1963

The east end of Bournemouth Central (as it was then called) has been a favourite location for photographs over the years, and there was the additional attraction of seeing engines struggle to get to grips with the rails on wet days, due to the sharp curve and short 1 in 150 gradient. This seemed to apply particularly to the Bulleid 'Pacifics'. Here on a fine day rebuilt 'Merchant Navy' No 35019 *French Line C.G.T.* is at the head of a Waterloo express. It entered service in June 1948 as No 21C19 just after nationalisation, was rebuilt in 1959 and withdrawn in September 1965, 53,000 short of a million miles in service. 9 June 1962

Bournemouth: the station and shed area

The Great Western 'Hall' and 'Grange' Classes were frequent visitors to Bournemouth in the mid-1960s, operating cross-country services from the north, usually taking over at Oxford. Normally the engine would stay overnight at Bournemouth and return the following day, hardly an intensive diagram compared with the 1,000-mile diagrams of CrossCountry 'Voyagers' today. Well-cleaned 'Modified Hall' No 7910 *Hown Hall* rests on the shed, carrying the 81C shed code that indicates it is a Southall engine. 10 June 1962

Possibly the best known of the Bulleid 'Battle of Britain' 'Pacifics' was No 34051 (originally 21C151) because of its name, *Winston Churchill*. It is now in the National Collection, where it is kept in immaculate external condition compared with how it appears in this photograph. New in December 1946, it remained in service until September 1965 and is credited with 807,496 miles in service. 28 October 1962

Bournemouth: the station and shed area

Bournemouth shed had an allocation of Class 'M7' 0-4-4Ts for decades. Back in 1950 14 were allocated, and they were used on local services on the Bournemouth avoiding line to Ringwood and especially the Swanage branch in push-pull mode. Here we see a line-up of five them on shed, Nos 30127, 30108, 30328, 30107 and 30111. No 30111 had been part of the shed's allocation 12 years earlier. 27 October 1962

Above: BR Standard 4MT No 75067 leaves the east end of Central station on an up local train. It was new to Dover shed in September 1955 and was allocated throughout the Southern Region, ending its career at Eastleigh shed in October 1964. Like all the 15 members of the class allocated to the Southern, when new it was fitted with a BR1B high-water-capacity tender (4,725 gallons) due to there being no water troughs. Again, as with all those sent new to the region it was modified with a double blastpipe chimney, on 3 December 1960. 9 June 1963

Right: This is a rear view of rebuilt 'Merchant Navy' No 35010 *Blue Star*, which was new as No 21C10 in July 1962, was rebuilt in late 1956 and continued in service until September 1966, being credited with 1,241,299 miles in service before passing into preservation. There was no problem in getting around the shed on Christmas Day. 25 December 1964

Bournemouth: the station and shed area

Bournemouth station has a very long down platform where trains can be split and depart separately. This has been a big advantage over the years as many of the expresses divided here, with a portion to Weymouth and another to Bournemouth West. 'Battle of Britain' No 34058 (21C158) *Sir Frederick Pile* has crossed over to what was then the through centre road and is heading west, with the steam shed building on the left. New in April 1947, No 34058 was rebuilt as late as September 1960 and withdrawn in October 1964, having only covered 173,114 miles in rebuilt form. It then passed into preservation. 8 June 1963

A fine selection of rebuilt 'West Country' and 'Battle of Britain' 'Pacifics' outside the shed are seen from the station platform. They include, on the extreme right, No 34085 *501 Squadron* under repair; new in November 1948 and rebuilt in May 1960, it was withdrawn in September 1965. In front of it is No 34109 *Sir Trafford Leigh-Mallory*, new in May 1950, rebuilt in March 1961 with only 162,601 miles travelled, and withdrawn in September 1964 after just 14 years. No 34108 *Wincanton* (middle left) was new in April 1950, rebuilt in March 1961 and withdrawn in June 1967; it is interesting to see that No 34108 managed 90,000 miles more than No 34109 in roughly the same period. Behind No 34109 is No 34059 (21C159) *Sir Archibald Sinclair*, new in April 1947, rebuilt in March 1960, withdrawn in May 1966 and now preserved. Finally on the left is No 34040 (21C140) *Crewkerne*, new in September 1946, rebuilt in October 1960 and withdrawn in July 1967, having only averaged around 36,000 miles per annum. How times have changed! 13 September 1964

Bournemouth: the station and shed area

Right: No 34057 (21C157) *Biggin Hill* is not carrying a shedplate but was allocated to Salisbury shed. It is in terrible external condition, which was unusual for that shed, but at least it is still carrying its nameplate. 18 April 1965

Below: Another view at the extreme west end of the station shows No 34077 *603 Squadron* in the platform road waiting to depart west. It entered traffic in July 1948, was rebuilt in May 1960 and withdrawn in March 1963. It covered around double the mileage of No 34058 in rebuilt form in around the same time. 8 June 1963

By this date the Ivatt 2-6-2Ts were a regular part of the steam scene in the area. Eastleigh Works was carrying out overhauls of the class together with the BR Standard classes, other than the 'Pacifics', and No 41283 has just received attention there. It is seen taking water on the shed, possibly on its way back to Templecombe, where it was allocated. 8 September 1965

Bournemouth: the station and shed area

There must have many more attractive jobs in the Bournemouth area at this time than cleaning steam engines, and it must be hoped that 'Merchant Navy' No 35013 (21C13) *Blue Funnel* was in better mechanical condition than it appears externally as it waits to depart from Bournemouth Central for Waterloo. It lasted to the end of Southern steam and no doubt put up some of the fantastic last-month performances when 104mph and 106mph were achieved on separate occasions. Its total mileage is recorded as 1,114,658, averaging more than 50,000 miles per annum. 29 August 1965

Two rebuilt Bulleid 'Pacifics' are on the shed awaiting their next duties. 'Battle of Britain' No 34060 (21C160) *25 Squadron*, new in April 1947, rebuilt in November 1960 and withdrawn in June 1967, is alongside 'Merchant Navy' No 35014 (21C14) *Nederland Line*, new in February 1945, rebuilt in July 1956 and withdrawn in March 1967, having achieved 1,062,394 miles in service. Christmas Day, 1964

Just to the east of Bournemouth station, at the top of the 1 in 150 gradient out of the station, was the goods yard. One seldom sees pictures taken at this location, but here is 'West Country' No 34097 *Holsworthy* on an up express to Waterloo. It entered service in November 1949, was rebuilt in March 1961 and withdrawn in April 1966. 10 September 1965

'West Country' No 34104 *Bere Alston* is passing the signal box opposite the goods yard with a down Channel Islands boat train. This was the last locomotive of the class to be built at Eastleigh Works in April 1950. Rebuilding was done in May 1961 and it was withdrawn in June 1967. Its total career mileage was 678,853, averaging less than 40,000 miles per annum. 10 September 1965

Seen emerging from under the station roof, having arrived on the centre road with a down van and empty coaching stock train, is 'Battle of Britain' No 34053 *Sir Keith Park*, allocated to Bournemouth at the time. It was new back in January 1947, rebuilt in November 1958 and withdrawn in October 1965, passing into preservation. 1 September 1965

Now very active on Network Rail working specials, No 34046 (21C146) *Braunton* currently appears in immaculate external condition compared to back in 1965, when it was part of the Bournemouth allocation and is shown awaiting servicing. It entered service in November 1946, was rebuilt in February 1959 and withdrawn in October 1965, one month after this picture was taken, eventually passing into preservation. 8 September 1965

Bournemouth: the station and shed area

BR Standard 4MT No 75070 emerges from under the station roof and heads towards the shed for servicing. The engine had a short career from October 1955 to September 1966, based on the Southern Region of BR. 22 July 1966

Below: A very well cleaned 'West Country' for the period, No 34032 (21C132) *Camelford* is on the shed opposite classmate No 34021 (21C121) *Dartmoor*. No 34032 was allocated to Salisbury at the time, which probably explains its fine appearance. New in 1946, rebuilt in October 1960 and withdrawn in October 1966, it ran only 204,243 miles in rebuilt form. 20 March 1966

Above: This picture of 'Merchant Navy' No 35003 (21C3) *Royal Mail* working the local pick-up freight tender-first out of the yard, which most likely includes coal for the shed, seems very unusual. No 35003 was new in May 1948 and rebuilt in August 1959. It survived to the end of Southern steam, having accumulated 1,131,793 miles in 29 years. 10 September 1965

Bournemouth: the station and shed area

BR Standard 4MT 2-6-0 No 76009, built at Darlington in February 1953, was allocated to the Southern Region for its working career, which ended in July 1967 when it was allocated to Bournemouth. It is departing on the down line at the west end of the station. 22 July 1966

The Southern Region received 20 BR Standard 5MT 4-6-0s from new; they were Nos 73080 to 73089 and 73110 to 73119 with high-water-capacity tenders, and all received names. The Western Region eventually had surplus members of the class on its books, and they were also transferred to the Southern; they had tenders with a lower water capacity and were painted in BR lined green livery. Here ex-WR No 73029 is at the head of an up train ready to leave the station, its external condition hardly showing the green livery to advantage. Built in January 1952, it survived until the end of Southern steam. 22 July 1966

Bournemouth: the station and shed area

Ivatt 2-6-2T No 41238 is seen on carriage shunting duties around the station within days of being withdrawn from the Bournemouth allocation. 7 September 1964

No 34005 (21C105) was the first of the Bulleid 'light Pacifics' to be rebuilt back in June 1957, having entered service in May 1948. Here it is shown emerging from the main road bridge at the east end of Bournemouth station with a down express from Waterloo. Withdrawal was in October 1966. 22 July 1966

Bournemouth: the station and shed area

By 1966 the Southern Region-allocated Class 33s were well established over the area. Here No D6501 (later No 33002) approaches the station passing the steam shed at the west end and overtakes No D6573 (later 33055) on some empty coaches in the siding. 31 July 1966

'West Country' No 34096 *Trevone* is blowing off on the shed before moving forward and reversing on to the main line, probably to proceed light engine to Bournemouth West station to work an up express. It entered service in November 1949 and was rebuilt in April 1961 before being withdrawn in September 1964, with 'only' 211,046 miles covered as a rebuild in three years. 9 June 1963

Another view from the west end of the down platform shows 'West Country' No 34091 *Weymouth*. Its working life was from September 1949 to September 1964, and it only covered 469,073 miles in its 15 years; it was only ever allocated to Stewarts Lane and Salisbury sheds. 7 September 1964

Above: BR Standard 2-6-0 No 76016 is at the west end of the station passing the shed as it approaches with an up local service. It had a short career of 13 years, being built at Doncaster in May 1953 and allocated to Guildford for all but its last four months of service; withdrawal came in October 1966. 9 September 1964

Right: 'Battle of Britain' No 34064 (21C164) *Fighter Command* was unique in the class, being not only the 1,000th locomotive to be built at Brighton Works but also the only 'Battle of Britain' to be fitted with a Giesl ejector and spark arrester during BR steam days – No 34092 *City of Wells* was modified in preservation. The modification is said to have improved the performance considerably, but it was not repeated as the end of steam was in sight. Here it is arriving with a portion of an up express for Waterloo. It achieved a modest total mileage of 759,666 before being withdrawn in November 1966. 22 May 1966

In the latter days of steam around the country the working conditions around most sheds can only be described as terrible and in many cases dangerous. It was little wonder that the railways found it so difficult to recruit. Bournemouth shed appeared to be no better than most, especially around the ashpit and primitive coaling facilities. These pictures illustrate the point. Standard 4MT 2-6-4T No 80146 (seen in both views) and Standard 5MT No 73117, named *Vivien*, stand in the servicing area, with Standard 4MT Nos 76057 and 76033 beyond. 31 July 1966

This shot, taken during the afternoon of Christmas Day 1966, again shows the piles of ash, some of it still burning, and not a soul to be seen at the shed. There are three 'Merchant Navies' on view: Nos 35026 *Lamport & Holt Line*, 35014 *Nederland Line* and 35028 *Clan Line*, the latter now preserved. 25 December 1966

Just outside the shed are 'West Country' Nos 34044 (21C144) *Woolacombe* and 34047 (21C147) *Callington*. Both entered service within a month of each other in October 1946 and were rebuilt in May 1960 and November 1958 respectively. Withdrawal for *Woolacombe* was in May 1967 and for *Callington* in June 1967. 25 December 1966

After six years of service No D6501 (later Class 33 No 33002) is looking smart in its BR green livery at the east end of Central station on an up express for Waterloo. It was the second member of the class to enter service, on 27 February 1960, was withdrawn on 13 February 1997, and was bought by Harry Needle. 31 July 1966

Initially three Brush Type 4s were allocated to services between Waterloo and Bournemouth, and one diagram usually included the 'Bournemouth Belle' Pullman train. No D1923 (later numbered 47246 and 47644) was one of the trio, and is seen on the shed in the company of 'Merchant Navy' No 35013 *Blue Funnel* again and Standard 5MT No 73092 in BR lined green livery; the latter engine was new in October 1955 and was withdrawn from Guildford in July 1967. 26 March 1967

A closer view of Nos 35013 and 73092 side by side. 26 March 1967

In another view from the down station platform we see 'Merchant Navy' No 35021 *New Zealand Line* on the shed. It entered traffic on 11 September 1948, was rebuilt in June 1959 and withdrawn in August 1965, having spent its last eight years allocated to Bournemouth. 10 September 1964

Bournemouth: the station and shed area

In commendably clean condition, 'West Country' No 34040 (21C140) *Crewkerne* is backing off the shed to work an up express. This loco was new in September 1946, rebuilt in October 1960 and withdrawn in July 1967, having been allocated to Bournemouth for its last 11 years. 10 September 1964

'Battle of Britain' No 34085 *501 Squadron* is under repair on the shed. Entering service in October 1948, it was rebuilt in June 1960 and withdrawn in September 1965. The total mileage for its 17-year career was 661,415, averaging just under 39,000 miles per year. 10 September 1964

Bournemouth: the station and shed area

'Battle of Britain' No 34059 (21C159) *Sir Archibald Sinclair* is on the shed turntable, which was situated at the extreme east end of the shed yard. The engine's details are given on page 12. 13 September 1964

'Battle of Britain' No 34087 *145 Squadron* bursts out of the bridge carrying the main road over the tracks at the east end of the station while tackling the short 1 in 150 gradient with an up express. The engine was new in December 1948, rebuilt in December 1960 and withdrawn on 9 July 1967. 12 September 1964

Another view of Ivatt 2-6-2T No 41238 in the station (see page 23) working out its last working days on stock movement duties. 20 September 1964

Ivatt 4MT 2-6-0 No 43019 is on the shed after a running-in turn from Eastleigh following a visit to the works. It is a very long way from its home shed of Lower Darwen near Blackburn. The initial batch of this class was built by the LMS at Horwich Works. No 43019 entered service in June 1948 and, after periods of being stored serviceable, was withdrawn in May 1968. 8 September 1965

Bournemouth: the station and shed area

Another view of Ivatt 2-6-2T No 41238 in the station (see page 23) working out its last working days on stock movement duties. 20 September 1964

No D6520 is in the BR Corporate Blue livery but has not yet received its TOPS number, 33107. As can be seen, it was one of the members of the class to be fitted for push-pull working between Bournemouth and Weymouth. It entered service on 3 September 1960 and is seen on an up Waterloo express at the east end of Central station. Withdrawal came prematurely after a bad accident on 20 April 1989 between Poole and Wareham. It was eventually scrapped at Springburn Works, Glasgow, in May 1991. 29 March 1967

Bournemouth: the station and shed area

This picture, taken well over a year before steam ended, shows the obvious problem of ash disposal at the shed. Stanier Class 5 No 44710 together with a BR 4MT and a Bulleid 'light Pacific' are lined up awaiting servicing. By this date some of the cross-country services that were still steam-worked had Stanier Class 5 haulage. 20 March 1966

Unrebuilt 'West Country' No 34102 *Lapford* is under repair at the shed. It entered service in March 1950 and was one of the last unrebuilt examples to remain in service, being withdrawn on 9 July 1967; it had covered a modest mileage of 593,438 miles in 17 years, an average of just under 35,000 miles per annum. 27 March 1967

Ivatt 4MT 2-6-0 No 43019 is on the shed after a running-in turn from Eastleigh following a visit to the works. It is a very long way from its home shed of Lower Darwen near Blackburn. The initial batch of this class was built by the LMS at Horwich Works. No 43019 entered service in June 1948 and, after periods of being stored serviceable, was withdrawn in May 1968. 8 September 1965

Note the terrible external condition of 'West Country' No 34023 (21C123) *Blackmore Vale*. It actually became the last unrebuilt Bulleid 'light Pacific' and survived to the end of Southern steam; it was much in demand during the last weeks and was involved in rail tours. New in March 1946, it covered 921,268 miles during its 21 years of service. It passed into preservation on the Bluebell Railway, where it has been a firm favourite ever since. 20 March 1966

By the date of this photograph what had now become the Class 33s were regular performers on the Waterloo services. No 33001 has received the BR Corporate Blue livery and is shown leaving with an up express with the new EMU coaches for the electric services. 29 March 1967

Bournemouth: the station and shed area

This rear view of 'Merchant Navy' No 35019 (21C19) *French Line C.G.T.* at the head of an up Waterloo express ready to leave also shows the fine signals at the east end of the up platform. The locomotive details are on page 6. 20 September 1964

The electric services had been in operation for more than 11 years by the time this picture of REP EMU No 3013 was taken, showing it leaving on a Waterloo service. 16 April 1979

Bournemouth: the station and shed area

One of the Class 33s that were modified for push-pull working, and classified as 33/1s, is arriving at the station heading an up Channel Islands boat train. It is interesting to see how the background has changed from steam days, as the Bournemouth ring road now runs over the top of where the shed once stood, and underneath is now a large station car park. 21 July 1979

Another view of a REP EMU leaving Bournemouth for Waterloo. With 3,300hp, these were the most powerful EMUs in service. 16 April 1979

Bournemouth: the station and shed area

Specials to Bournemouth from outside the region were normally hauled by the Brush Type 4s, later Class 47s. This special is for Wolverhampton and has No 47315 at the head, one of the 81 members of the class not fitted for train heating, which was quite usual in the summer months. Other '47' duties for the class included cross-country trains that had been diverted away from the Somerset & Dorset line in the mid-1960s. 16 April 1979

These two pictures show the locomotive changeover from diesel to electric traction at Bournemouth for up Channel Islands boat trains. On this day Class 33/1 No 33113 has brought the train from Weymouth and Class 73 No 73131, in the then new BR 'Large Logo' livery, is taking over. The electro-diesel, built in 1966, was withdrawn in 2003, while the '33' entered service in November 1960 and lasted until October 1992, about double the length of service compared to some Bulleid 'Pacifics' and BR Standard classes. 3 August 1985

Bournemouth: the station and shed area

The locomotive changeover for the boat trains involved both platforms. Class 33/1 No 33113 is now on the down side behind an EMU, while No 73131 is ready to depart from the up side. 3 August 1985

Here is another of the interesting dual-powered Class 73s, in ex-works condition at the head of an up Channel Islands boat train that had arrived from Weymouth behind a Class 33/1. This particular member of the class entered service in 1966 and lasted until 2003. The class is still active today, with some having had extensive rebuilding with Caterpillar engines and working the sleeper services in Scotland. 21 July 1979

A Virgin CrossCountry HST headed by Class 43 No 43065 makes a smoky departure forming the 14.17 service to Manchester Piccadilly. A Class 442 EMU is on the left. Both are very colourful examples of the liveries introduced at sectorisation. 12 September 1992

Bournemouth: the station and shed area

Most of the Class 73s received the 'Large Logo' InterCity livery for the 'Gatwick Express' services, and in the later 1980s they were regularly employed on the Waterloo- Bournemouth services in push-pull mode. On a day showing that the sun does not always shine in Bournemouth, No 73103 is unusually at the rear of the TC coaches for a trip to Waterloo. This loco was new in 1965 and, after extensive rebuilding involving the installation of a Caterpillar engine and the removal of all third rail equipment, has now started an entirely new career working in Scotland for the Caledonian Sleeper services, renumbered 73970. 18 March 1988

Class 47/4 No 47638 arrives at the station with a Newcastle-Poole cross-country express. The locomotive was new in February 1965 and carried the numbers D1653, 47069, 47638 and 47845 during its career to October 2001, then 57301 when it was converted to a Class 57. It also carried the name *County of Kent* between June 1996 and September 2001. 18 March 1988

Bournemouth: the station and shed area

An everyday scene at the turn of the 20th century was the sight of the Class 442 'Wessex Electrics' on the Waterloo services. Here No 2421 is being boarded. 17 November 2001

Class 73/1 No 73126 in InterCity livery carries out an empty stock movement from the down to the up platform to form an express to Waterloo. This loco was originally numbered E6033 and was named *Kent & East Sussex Railway* between May 1994 and July 1997. It entered service in May 1966 and was withdrawn in January 1999. 18 March 1988

Bournemouth: the station and shed area

The 'Dorset Scot' HST service is seen in the station with power car No 43088 at the rear before departing for the north. 17 November 2001

At the other end of the 'Dorset Scot' is power car No 43166, pulling away from the east end of the station. 17 November 2001

Bournemouth: the station and shed area

When the famous Class 442s were withdrawn from the Bournemouth services they were redeployed on the 'Gatwick Express' trains. After withdrawal from those duties they were placed into store, but are currently being overhauled to work on the Waterloo-Portsmouth services. Here unit No 2414 is seen from the west end of the station before leaving for Waterloo. 17 November 2001

What a difference 34 years makes – where once there were mountains of ash and coal and working conditions most people today would not believe existed, now the car park is surrounded by colourful autumn trees to match the very attractive South West Trains colour scheme applied to Class 442 EMU No 2414. 17 November 2001

Bournemouth: the station and shed area

Fares for the shuttle train for a Bournemouth Open Day. 12 September 1992

Bournemouth shed codes (BR)

71B, 1950-63
70F, 1963-67

Bournemouth shed allocation in 1950

'M7' 0-4-4T	14
'B4' 0-4-0T	3
'O2s' 0-4-4T	2
'G6' 0-6-0T	1
'Q' 0-6-0	2
'S11' 4-4-0	3
'700' 0-6-0	1
'T9' 4-4-0 1 'King Arthur' 4-6-0	9
'Lord Nelson' 4-6-0	5
'U' 2-6-0 3	
'West Country' 4-6-2	7
'Battle of Britain' 4-6-2	1
Total	52

Bournemouth shed allocation in 1959

'M7' 0-4-4T	16
'B4' 0-4-0T	2
'G6' 0-6-0T	1
'T9' 4-4-0	3
'Q' 0-6-0	3
'700' 0-6-0	2
'King Arthur' 4-6-0	7
'Lord Nelson' 4-6-0	3
'U' 2-6-0 3	
'West Country' 4-6-2	13
'Battle of Britain' 4-6-2	7
Total	60

Bournemouth shed allocation in 1965

'West Country' 4-6-2	5
'Battle of Britain' 4-6-2	2
'Merchant Navy' 4-6-2	9
Ivatt 2MT 2-6-2T	8
BR 4MT 2-6-0	8
BR 4MT 2-6-4T	7
Total	39

Further reading:

Railways & Recollections
No 100 The Somerset & Dorset
Railway 1961-66

Prior to closure in 1967 Bournemouth West station had been served by trains running down the Somerset & Dorset line from Bath Green Park, until it too closed on 7 March 1966.

In this volume Gavin Morrison gives a photographic glimpse into the workings of the Somerset & Dorset line in its last six years. Unfortunately he did not have the opportunity to see it in earlier years, although its 114 miles have probably had almost as much photographic coverage as the Settle & Carlisle or West Highland lines.

The S&D, as it became known – also, affectionately, as the 'Slow and Dirty' – was created in 1862 by the amalgamation of the Somerset Central Railway and the Dorset Central Railway, which seemed to continually struggle financially in spite of what appeared on paper to be worthwhile expansions. Eventually the company went into receivership in 1875, resulting in a 999-year lease agreement jointly with the Midland Railway and the London & South Western Railway.

After the Grouping it was jointly operated by the London Midland & Scottish Railway and the Southern Railway. Following nationalisation it passed to the Southern Region of BR and, in its last few years, to the Western Region, which implemented the closure.

ISBN: 978 1 85794 539 3   64 pages   £8.00

Index of Locomotive Classes

Steam

'Black 5' 4-6-0	41
BR 4MT 2-6-0	10, 19, 21, 22, 27
BR 4MT 2-6-4T	28
BR 5MT 4-6-0	33
Ivatt 2MT 2-6-2T	14, 23, 39
Ivatt 4MT 2-6-0	42
'M7' 0-4-4T	9
'Merchant Navy' 4-6-2	5, 6, 10, 15, 20, 32, 33, 34, 45
'Modified Hall' 4-6-0	7
'Q' 0-6-0	4
'West Country'/'Battle of Britain' 4-6-2	5, 8, 11, 12, 13, 16, 17, 18, 20, 24, 26, 27, 29, 31, 35, 36, 37

Diesel/electro-diesel

Class 33	3, 25, 30, 40, 44, 47, 50, 52
Class 43 HST	54, 56, 60, 61
Class 47	33, 49, 56
Class 73	50, 51, 52, 53, 55, 57

Electric multiple units

Class 442	54, 56, 60, 61
REP	46-48